GW00686333

Francis Frith's **50**
CLASSICS

BEAUTIFUL
VILLAGES

The Francis Frith Collection

First published in the United Kingdom in 2004 by
Frith Book Company Ltd

ISBN 1-85937-902-8

British Library Cataloguing in Publication Data

Francis Frith's 50 Classics - Beautiful Villages
Compiled by Terence Sackett and Julia Skinner

Frith Book Company Ltd
Frith's Barn, Teffont,
Salisbury, Wiltshire SP3 5QP
Tel: +44 (0) 1722 716 376
Email: info@francisfrith.co.uk
www.francisfrith.co.uk

Printed and bound in Great Britain

Front Cover: WEARE GIFFARD, The Post Office 1923 75118
The colour-tinting is for illustrative purposes only, and is not intended to be historically accurate.

AS WITH ANY HISTORICAL DATABASE THE FRITH ARCHIVE IS CONSTANTLY BEING
CORRECTED AND IMPROVED AND THE PUBLISHERS WOULD WELCOME INFORMATION
ON OMISSIONS OR INACCURACIES

FRANCIS FRITH
VICTORIAN PIONEER

Francis Frith, founder of the world-famous photographic archive, was a complex and multi-talented man. A devout Quaker and a highly successful Victorian businessman, he was philosophic by nature and pioneering in outlook. By 1855 he had already established a wholesale grocery business in Liverpool, and sold it for the astonishing sum of £200,000, which is the equivalent today of over £15,000,000. Now in his thirties, and captivated by the new science of photography, Frith set out on a series of pioneering journeys up the Nile and to the Near East.

INTRIGUE AND EXPLORATION
He was the first photographer to venture beyond the sixth cataract of the Nile. Africa was still the mysterious 'Dark Continent', and Stanley and Livingstone's historic meeting was a decade into the future. The conditions for picture taking confound belief. He laboured for hours in his wicker dark-room in the sweltering heat of the desert, while the volatile chemicals fizzed dangerously in their trays. Back in London he exhibited his photographs and was 'rapturously cheered' by members of the Royal Society. His reputation as a photographer was made overnight.

VENTURE OF A LIFE-TIME
By the 1870s the railways had threaded their way across the country, and Bank Holidays and half-day Saturdays had been made obligatory by Act of Parliament. All of a sudden the working man and his family were able to enjoy days out, take holidays, and see a little more of the world.

With typical business acumen, Francis Frith foresaw that these new tourists would enjoy having souvenirs to commemorate their days out. For the next thirty years he travelled the country by train and by pony and trap, producing fine photographs of seaside resorts and beauty spots that were keenly bought by millions of Victorians.

These prints were painstakingly pasted into family albums and pored over during the dark nights of winter, rekindling precious memories of summer excursions. Frith's studio was soon supplying retail shops all over the country, and by 1890 F Frith & Co had become the greatest specialist photographic publishing company in the world, with over 2,000 sales outlets, and pioneered the picture postcard.

FRANCIS FRITH'S LEGACY

Francis Frith had died in 1898 at his villa in Cannes, his great project still growing. The archive he created continued in business for another seventy years. By 1970 it contained over a third of a million pictures showing 7,000 British towns and villages.

Frith's legacy to us today is of immense significance and value, for the magnificent archive of evocative photographs he created provides a unique record of change in the cities, towns and villages throughout Britain over a century and more. Frith and his fellow studio photographers revisited locations many times down the years to update their views, compiling for us an enthralling and colourful pageant of British life and character.

We are fortunate that Frith was dedicated to recording the minutiae of everyday life. For it is this sheer wealth of visual data, the painstaking chronicle of changes in dress, transport, street layouts, buildings, housing, engineering and landscape that captivates us so much today, offering us a powerful link with the past and with the lives of our ancestors.

Computers have now made it possible for Frith's many thousands of images to be accessed almost instantly. The archive offers every one of us an opportunity to examine the places where we and our families have lived and worked down the years. Its images, depicting our shared past, are now bringing pleasure and enlightenment to millions around the world a century and more after his death.

INTRODUCTION

This pocket book is one of a series of photographic anthologies of subjects and themes from British life, history and heritage.

This colourful pocket book contains 50 classic Frith photographs of picturesque village scenes from all over England.

You'll find beautiful cottages in a wide variety of regional styles and materials including half-timbering, cob, stone, brick, thatch, tile, and slate; here you'll see mills, inns, churches and village greens; you can watch children at play and village people chatting or going about their daily lives. Each photograph is accompanied by an informative caption.

Evocative and atmospheric, these stunning images will transport you back into a charming rural idyll.

All Stretton lies between the Long Mynd and Carodoc. Nearby is the Cwm Spring supplying mineral water which is bottled in the village.

The ford that gave Allerford its name lies beside an ancient, two-arched packhorse bridge. The village's thatched former schoolhouse is now home to the West Somerset Museum of Rural Life, which gives a fascinating insight into the daily lives of people in the area not that long ago.

ALLERFORD, SOMERSET 1923   75023

Axmouth, in East Devon, was an important port until its river entrance silted up. The early Norman church of St Michael was altered and enlarged in 1330, and a perpendicular tower was added in the 15th century.

Lying about ten miles east of Hawes, Aysgarth is famous for a series of waterfalls on the River Ure, the upper of which can still be viewed from a 16th-century single arched bridge. The village became popular with visitors to the falls.

AYSGARTH, YORKSHIRE 1908 60790

9

Boscastle's rugged harbour is a romantic inlet, twisting and turning for half a mile between brooding cliffs of slate and shale. Hawsers 'thick as a man's thigh' check the impetus of boats entering on the tide.

Now in effect a suburb of Taunton, the village has a 1586 Elizabethan manor house. The church of St Peter and St Paul is unusual in having one of Somerset's octagonal towers. Since 1906, the cottage on the left has gone, and the church porch has been rebuilt.

BISHOP'S HULL, SOMERSET 1906 55810

11

'The Biggest Village in Devon' is how Braunton likes to be known. The original St Brannock's Church in the village was built after the Irish saint had a dream that he must build a church where he discovered a sow and piglets. This was the place.

BRAUNTON, DEVON 1900 45685

Both Charles I and Oliver Cromwell stayed in the village during the Civil War. A number of the older houses in Broadway were originally inns, for the village lay on the London to Worcester coaching route.

Byworth is a pretty village with a single winding street a mile east of Petworth; it is set on hilly ground above a small stream flowing in a steep valley towards the Rother. These two timber-framed houses were originally built for prosperous farmers; in Victorian times the houses were each subdivided into labourers' cottages for the Leconfield Estate.

BYWORTH, SUSSEX 1906 54367

Cadgwith is one of Cornwall's prettiest fishing villages, and huddles between steep cliffs a few miles north of the Lizard. Crabbing is a local industry.

Cartmel has been described as a cathedral city in miniature. The magnificent late 12th-century priory church of St Mary and St Michael was founded in 1190 by William Marshall, Baron of Cartmel. It was a priory of the Augustinian Order, and still serves as the parish church.

CARTMEL, CUMBRIA 1914 67406

In the backgound are the ruins of Bolton Castle, which was built by Richard Scrope in the 1380s. Though designed as a fortress, the castle's principal function appears to have been residential; it was one of the first to have chimneys. Mary Queen of Scots was imprisoned here for six months, and the castle was partly dismantled at the end of the Civil War. It was then used by local families, who lived in tenements built within the walls; the last of these left in 1898.

◀ *Castle Combe was once a centre for cloth weaving. The steep stone roofs of the houses are typical of Cotswold villages.*

▶ *The Frome Valley, dotted with mills and with the Thames and Severn Canal running through it, has long been a centre of the cloth industry. Chalford itself stands on the steep north bank. Many of the wealthy clothiers' 19th-century houses were built on terraces cut into the hillside, with the result that the front doors are several storeys above the garden entrance.*

CHALFORD, GLOS. 1910 62713

19

If Sally Spencer, the lady in the photograph, came back today, she would see that almost all in this view has been demolished since 1908, partly for road widening to cope with Cheddar's enormous volume of tourists.

CHEDDAR, SOMERSET 1908 60144

The village of Cookham is famous for the colourful tradition of swan-upping, which dates from time immemorial and involves the swans being upped, or counted, classified and marked. The Queen's swans are unmarked.

The Asshetons, who first became squires here in 1559, have been keen to keep Downham's appearance unspoiled, and in more recent times have had the electric cables buried underground. The picturesque village has been used for the filming of the BBC series 'Born and Bred'.

East Barsham's manor house was built by Sir William Fermor during the reign of Henry VII. Henry VIII was a guest there, and walked 2 miles barefoot to the shrine at Walsingham.

EAST BARSHAM, NORFOLK

1929   82041

23

◀ *This village was once known as Clandon Abbots, for its manor, as in many other Surrey villages, was owned by the local abbey. Here, Chertsey Abbey owned the manor from about AD666.*

▶ *Elstead boasts a medieval bridge over the River Wey, and a triangular village green. An oak tree on the green was planted in 1897 for Queen Victoria's diamond jubilee.*

ELSTEAD, SURREY 1906 55623

One of the rectors of Eversley was Charles Kingsley, who wrote 'The Water Babies' whilst he lived there; Kingsley and his wife are buried in the churchyard.

EVERSLEY, HAMPSHIRE 1906 57011

This charming and ancient market town, between the Kent Estuary and Cartmel Sands, takes its name from Floki, the name of a Norse settler. It was renowned for its cockle gatherers and fishing for flukes, or flat fish, in the estuary.

Situated on Frensham Common, and spanning 108 acres, two fishponds were constructed in the 13th century to supply fish for the Bishops of Worcester, who were then residing in Farnham Castle.

FRENSHAM, SURREY 1914 67551A

The Cross in Geddington's village centre was built in 1294 to commemorate Queen Eleanor of Castile, the beloved wife of Edward I. The memorial is one of 12 original crosses representing resting places on the route of her funeral procession to Westminster Abbey in 1290. Only three remain: the other two are at Hardingstone, near Northampton, and Waltham Cross in Hertfordshire. The cross contains small statues of the Queen.

St Mary's churchyard in Gisburn contains an unusual headstone, that of Jenny Preston, showing a witch with her cauldron. Oliver Cromwell stabled horses and troops in the church after the Battle of Preston in 1648.

Gnosall's church of St Lawrence is largely 13th century, with some fine Norman details and an impressive central tower. Nearby is the former village lock-up, built in 1830, and moved to its present position from its original site in the village street.

GNOSALL, STAFFORSHIRE 1899 44334

31

This beautiful village is set up on a hilltop, surrounded by orchards and hopfields. St Mary's Church was founded in the 14th century, with its tower built in 1640. It crowns the hill, and has many monuments to the Culpeper family.

The village church is immortalised in the last two lines of Rupert Brooke's poem 'The Old Vicarage, Grantchester': 'Stands the church clock at five to three And is there honey still for tea?' It is believed that the clock was actually broken when the poet was living in Grantchester. For years after Brooke's death in the First World War, the clock was kept at that time as a memorial to him.

GRANTCHESTER, CAMBRIDGESHIRE

1929   81768

33

Grassington was once a centre for lead-mining, but by 1900 relied on agriculture and quarrying. In 1902 the railway came to the village, with the opening of a line to Skipton.

At 42 acres, Great Bentley's village green is the largest in England. Its steam mill was built in 1886, and lasted until 1925, when the chimney was demolished.

GREAT BENTLEY, ESSEX 1902
48290

35

Charlotte Bronte stayed at the vicarage of the hillside town on Hathersage in 1845; the rector Henry Nussey proposed to her but she declined him. Charlotte's novel 'Jane Eyre' is set around the area, Hathersage appearing in the book under the name of Morton.

Kempsey's church has a puzzling 8th-century monument inside, which reads: 'Underneath the corruptible parts of a vicar, one husband, two helpmeets, both wives and both Anns, a triplicity of persons in two twains but one flesh, are interred'.

KEMPSEY, HEREFORD AND WORCESTER
1910   62358

37

IGHTHAM, KENT 1901 47623

Ightham is a lovely old village of half-timbered cottages and houses, with a 14th-century church. Nearby is Ightham Mote, a famous secluded medieval manor house with a 15th-century great hall, an old chapel and a crypt.

Kenilworth is famous for its castle. The first castle built here is thought to have been a motte and bailey constructed between 1122-1127 by Geoffrey de Clinton. One of Kenilworth's prisoners was the deposed Edward II, who was held here prior to his transfer to Berkeley Castle , where he was murdered with a red hot poker.

Liphook expanded as a village thanks to the London-Portsmouth road and the arrival of the railway in 1859. The journey from the capital to the naval port by coach took eight hours: the six hours to Liphook cost 13s 6d. Samuel Pepys visited the Royal Anchor Hotel, originally a posting and coaching house, and found 'good, honest people' there.

LIPHOOK, HAMPSHIRE 1911 63110

MAIDEN NEWTON, DORSET 1906 54563

The working lives of the Dorset labourers who lived in cottages like these were hard, with poor wages and long hours. Although picturesque, the cottages were damp, unhealthy and overcrowded. One of Thomas Hardy's few forays into politics was to champion the cause of better treatment for rural workers.

Melplash's only real claim to fame is the story of Sir Thomas More (a distant relative of the saint): when he was sheriff of Dorset he freed all the prisoners from Dorchester gaol. More had to give both Melplash and his favourite daughter to Lord Paulet, who interceded with the king on his behalf in search of a pardon.

A former vicar of Monkland, Sir Henry Baker, wrote many hymns and was a compiler of 'Hymns Ancient and Modern'. The man standing outside the pub in this photograph is a postman; at this date there were often three postal deliveries a day.

Evesham Abbey held the Manor of Ombersley for several centuries until the Dissolution, its abbots often residing there. In the early 17th century it came into the possession of the Sandys family. Three veterans of Waterloo are commemorated in the church, including Lord Sandys, aide-de-camp of Lord Wellington.

Henry II's great 12th century keep stands sentinel over Orford, built to guard the coast where Flemish mercenaries were brought ashore by the Earl of Norfolk, whose castles far out-numbered royal castles in East Anglia. Across the river from Orford are some of the defence installations built on Orford Ness during the First World War. During the Second World War, Orford Ness was used by the scientist Robert Watson-Watt to develop radar.

ORFORD, SUFFOLK 1909 62015

47

On the right is the half-timbered Priest's House, which is thought to date from the 14th century. Above the entrance is a gallery and it was from here that a parson, ejected from the church by the Commonwealth, used to preach to the villagers. The house later became a bank.

Thomas Babington Macaulay, Rothley's most famous son, was born at Rothley Temple on St Crispin's Day, 1800, the son of the anti-slaver, Zachary Macaulay. Thomas became the Whig MP for Calne, Leeds, but it was his masterpiece - 'A History of England', that brought him fame.

ROTHLEY, LEICS c1955 R259001

49

50

The cottages on the right were almshouses (now gone). The white house just past them is known as the Penthouse - a name connected with the fact that the village pound (or pent) for stray cattle once stood here.

This beautiful Thames-side village was once a palace of the Bishops of Salisbury. The Deanery, one of Sonning's most famous buildings, was built for Edward Hudson, the owner of 'Country Life', in 1901, and designed by Sir Edwin Lutyens. The village was also the home of Dick Turpin's aunt.

The church of St James in Stanstead Abbots contains a monument to Sir Felix Booth (1775-1850); in 1829 he set out in the 'Endeavour' to find the North-West Passage, but discovered instead the magnetic north pole.

STANSTEAD ABBOTS, HERTS 1929 81859

53

This is a typical Nottinghamshire brick tower mill, tall and black-tarred. The photograph shows the mill in full working order. It was built in 1825, and ceased work by wind in about 1930 and by engine in 1940; the cap was removed in 1934. It is now converted to a private house.

The church of St James the Great in Twycross contains the oldest stained glass in England, which is originally French - it was made in Paris in around 1145.

TWYCROSS, LEICS c1960 T237006

55

◀ *Many years before Wargrave grew in popularity as a riverside village, Edith, wife of Edward the Confessor, held the manor, and at that time it was known as 'Weregrave'.*

▶ *The village green is overlooked by the Bell Inn. Just beyond the Inn is an area known as the 'fishermen's flats' (these days a car park), where the fishermen laid out their nets on trestles to dry.*

WALBERSWICK, SUFFOLK
1919   69128

57

Wooburn Green, in the valley of the River Wye, has a delightful green, and, to the south, the site of a moated palace of the medieval bishops of Lincoln. Later in the early 18th century the Duke of Wharton created a vast mansion from the palace. The remnants were demolished in 1964 and replaced by a housing estate.

INDEX

FREE PRINT OF YOUR CHOICE

Choose any Frith photograph in this book.
Simply complete the Voucher opposite and return it with your remittance for £2.25 (to cover postage and handling) and we will print the photograph of your choice in SEPIA (size 11 x 8 inches) and supply it in a cream mount with a burgundy rule line (overall size 14 x 11inches).
Please note: photographs with a reference number starting with a "Z" are not Frith photographs and cannot be supplied under this offer.
Offer valid for delivery to UK addresses only.

PLUS: **Order additional Mounted Prints at HALF PRICE - £7.49 each** (normally £14.99)
If you would like to order more Frith prints from this book, possibly as gifts for friends and family, you can buy them at half price (with no additional postage and handling costs).

PLUS: **Have your Mounted Prints framed**
For an extra £14.95 per print you can have your mounted print(s) framed in an elegant polished wood and gilt moulding, overall size 16 x 13inches (no additional postage and handling required).

FRITH PRODUCTS AND SERVICES

All Frith photographs are available for you to buy as framed or mounted prints. From time to time, other illustrated items such as Address Books, Calendars, Table Mats are also available. Already, almost 50,000 Frith archive photographs can be viewed and purchased on the internet through the Frith website.

For more detailed information on Frith companies and products, visit:

www.francisfrith.co.uk

Mounted Print
Overall size 14 x 11 inches (355 x 280mm)

IMPORTANT!

These special prices are only available if you use this form to order. You must use the ORIGINAL VOUCHER on this page (no copies permitted).

We can only despatch to one address. This offer cannot be combined with any other offer.

For further information, contact:
The Francis Frith Collection, Frith's Barn,
Teffont, Salisbury SP3 5QP
Tel: +44 (0) 1722 716 376
Fax: +44 (0) 1722 716 881
Email: sales@francisfrith.co.uk

Send completed Voucher form to:

UK and rest of world - The Francis Frith Collection, Frith's Barn, Teffont, Salisbury, Wiltshire SP3 5QP England

If you need more space, please write your address on a separate sheet of paper.

Voucher

for FREE and Reduced Price Frith Prints

Do not photocopy this voucher. Only the original is valid, so please fill it in, cut it out and return it to us with your order.

Picture ref no	Page number	Qty	Mounted @ £7.49 UK	Framed + £14.95	UK orders Total £
1		1	Free of charge*	£	£
2			£7.49	£	£
3			£7.49	£	£
4			£7.49	£	£
5			£7.49	£	£
6			£7.49	£	£
			* Post & handling (UK)		£2.25
			Total Order Cost		£

Please allow 28 days for delivery

Title of this book ....

I enclose a cheque / postal order for £ ....
payable to 'The Francis Frith Collection'

OR debit my Mastercard / Visa / Switch (Maestro) / Amex card

(credit cards please on all overseas orders), details below

Card Number ....

Issue No (switch only)   Valid from (Amex/Switch)

Expires   Signature

Name Mr/Mrs/Ms ....

Address ....

.... Postcode ....

Daytime Tel No ....

E-mail ....

Valid to 31/12/07